Ins[illegible] Thoughts

VOLUME ONE

2nd Revised Edition

Ocean

Books

Ocean Books
18 Pentrich Avenue,
Enfield, Middlesex.
EN1 4LZ.
Tel (020) 8350 9600

Inspirational Thoughts

VOLUME ONE

2nd Revised Edition

A Compilation of wonderful quotations for your personal growth.

Tycho Photiou

The sources of quotations in this book are many and varied - there are quotations from various religious texts, particularly Buddhism and Christianity, and there are many quotations from wise men and women through the centuries including, and up to, the present day.

Some of the relatively modern sources are acknowledged in the bibliography. Whilst the publisher has made every effort to obtain permission for the quotations wherever appropriate, this may not have been possible in every case.

We would therefore like to thank everyone who provided the wonderful and rich teachings that you will find within these pages, and accept our apologies if any modern sources have not been adequately acknowledged.

2nd Edition - Published 2001

Printed in Great Britain by
Redwood Books Ltd, Kennet Way, Trowbridge,
Wiltshire, BA14 8RN.

You are a child
of the universe, no less
than the trees and the stars,
you have a right to be here.
And whether or not it
is clear to you, no doubt
the universe is unfolding
as it should.

MAX EHRMANN

Contents

You Are What You Think
4

Create The Life You Desire
11

Take Responsibility
27

Keep A Positive Attitude
32

Don't Judge - Love
43

Resolving Conflict
57

Learn from Life
65

Finding Inner Peace And Happiness
74

The Law Of Cause And Effect
86

Help Whoever You Can
96

Keep Smiling
106

Enjoy life - NOW!
114

Bibliography
122

You Are What You Think

A man becomes
what he thinks about
all day long.
RALPH WALDO EMERSON

Our inner thoughts, beliefs
and attitudes are causes,
our external circumstances
are effects.
TYCHO

Every good thought you think is contributing its share to the ultimate result of your life.

GRENVILLE KLEISER

You can think your way to failure and misery, but you can also think your way to success and happiness.

NORMAN VINCENT PEALE

If you think
kind, loving thoughts,
you will have
kind, loving relationships.

TYCHO

What we are today comes
from our thoughts of
yesterday, and our present
thoughts build our life of
tomorrow, our life is the
creation of our mind.

THE BUDDHA

Our self-image is the single most important factor in determining our success and happiness in life.

TYCHO

Some of your beliefs originated in your childhood, but you are not at their mercy unless you believe that you are.

JANE ROBERTS

The world in which we live
is not primarily determined
by outward conditions and
circumstances, but by the
thoughts that habitually
occupy the mind.

NORMAN VINCENT PEALE

It is not enough to
have a good mind.
The main thing is to know
how to use it.

RENÉ DESCARTES

Whether you believe that you can, or whether you believe that you can't, you are right

HENRY FORD

To believe a thing is impossible is to make it so.

FRENCH PROVERB

Create The Life You Desire

*Whatever you want to
create in your life,
you must first create in
your imagination.*

TYCHO

*It is through the imagination
that the formless takes form.*

CATHERINE PONDER

Whatever the mind can conceive and believe, it can achieve.

Napoleon Hill

Any idea seriously entertained tends to bring about the realisation of itself.

Joseph Chilton Pearce

The principle of life is that life responds by corresponding; your life becomes the thing you have decided it shall be.

RAYMOND CHARLES BARKER

Life is a self-fulfilling prophecy.

PROVERB

Every day holds just as much promise as we're capable of expecting.

KAREN CASEY / MARTHA VANCEBURG

Hold fast to dreams
for if dreams die,
life is a broken-winged bird
that cannot fly.

LANGSTON HUGHES

You always get what you expect, if you expect it for long enough.

TYCHO

If you can imagine it, you can achieve it. If you can dream it, you can become it.

WILLIAM ARTHUR WARD

No man knows what he
can do until he tries.

PUBLILIUS SYRUS

Every big accomplishment in
history has come about
by someone holding
to their vision.

TYCHO

To be what we are, and to
become what we are capable
of becoming is the
only end of life.

ROBERT LOUIS STEVENSON

The tragedy of life doesn't lie
in not reaching your goal.
The tragedy lies in having
no goal to reach.

BENJAMIN E. MAYS

The great thing in this world is not so much where we are, but in what direction we are moving.

OLIVER WENDELL HOLMES

Why build a shack for yourself in your imagination, when you could build a palace?

TYCHO

A man's reach should
exceed his grasp,
or what's a heaven for?

ROBERT BROWNING

The people who get on in
this world are the people
who get up and look for
the circumstances they want,
and, if they can't find
them, make them.

GEORGE BERNARD SHAW

No challenge is beyond our capability; Every challenge promises new growth and a measure of serenity.

KAREN CASEY / MARTHA VANCEBURG

Your limitations are created by what you believe your limitations are.

TYCHO

It is common sense to take a method and try it.
If it fails, admit it frankly and try another.
But above all, try something.

FRANKLIN D ROOSEVELT

Limited expectations yield only limited results.

SUSAN LAURSON WILLIG

We learn wisdom from failure much more than from success; We often discover what will do, by finding out what will not do; And probably he who never made a mistake, never made a discovery.

SAMUEL SMILES

There is no failure except in no longer trying.

ELBERT HUBBARD

You're not a failure if you don't make it; you're a success because you try.

Susan Jeffers

The only person who makes no mistakes is the person who does nothing, and that is the greatest mistake of all!

Dr William J. Reilly

Even if you're on the right track, you'll get run over if you just sit there.

WILL ROGERS

Winners never quit, quitters never win.

ANONYMOUS

However many holy words you read, however many you speak; what good will they do you, if you do not act upon them?

THE DHAMMAPADA

Ask for God's blessing on your work, but don't ask him to do it for you.

THOMAS ALLEN

Take Responsibility

When we finally
give up the struggle
to find fulfilment "out there",
we have nowhere to
go but within.

SHAKTI GAWAIN

Blame what you will but
nothing will change;
it's something inside that
you must rearrange.

ANDREA PHOTIOU

If we try too hard to force others to live in our world, because we think it is the real world, we are doomed to disappointment.

WILLIAM GLASER

The less you need to be in control, the greater will be your positive influence within your environment.

TYCHO

To wait for someone else, or
to expect someone else to
make my life richer, or fuller,
or more satisfying, puts me
in a constant state
of tension.

KATHLEEN TIERNEY ANDRUS

Your ability to make things happen, increases in direct proportion to your awareness that you have the ability to make things happen.

TYCHO

Keep A
Positive Attitude

I have learnt a lesson
from two of my friends,
who made me realise
on what happiness depends.
They both have exactly
equal things in life,
a job, a car, a home and a wife.
Yet one is happy the other is sad;
one thinks life is good,
the other thinks it's bad.
The difference is in their point of
view, and the way they look at
what they do.

TYCHO

It is the way we look at the scenery that needs changing, and not the scenery itself.

TYCHO

Your attitude determines your altitude.

ANONYMOUS

Every problem is
an outward manifestation of
our state of consciousness.
When our consciousness is
clear and at peace,
the problem disappears.

ARNOLD PATENT

You don't know what
you've got 'till it's gone.

PROVERB

When I look back on all these worries I remember the story of the old man who said on his deathbed that he had had a lot of trouble in his life, most of which had never happened.

WINSTON CHURCHILL

What a wonderful life I've had! I only wish I'd realised it sooner.

COLETTE

*Men are disturbed not by
things that happen,
but by their opinion of the
things that happen.*

EPICTETUS

*An optimist may see a light
where there is none, but why
must the pessimist always
run to blow it out?*

MICHEL DE SAINT-PIERRE

Keep your face to the sunshine and you cannot see the shadow.

ANONYMOUS

A man who fears suffering is already suffering from what he fears.

MICHEL DE MONTAIGNE

Sticks and stones may break my bones, but words can never hurt me......... unless I believe that they can.

ADAPTED PROVERB

Pain is inevitable. Suffering is optional.

M. KATHLEEN CASEY

*We are injured and hurt
emotionally, not so much by
other people or what they
say or don't say,
but by our own attitude
and our own response.*

MAXWELL MALTZ

*No one can make you feel
inferior without
your consent.*

ELEANOR ROOSEVELT

The quality of one's life depends on the quality of attention. Whatever you pay attention to will grow more important in your life.

DEEPAK CHOPRA

Where attention goes, energy flows.

JAMES REDFIELD / CAROL ADRIENNE

If you pay attention
to someone's generosity,
kindness and strength,
then they will become more
generous, kind and strong.

TYCHO

The best way to raise them
is always to praise them.

THOMAS ALLEN

Don't Judge - Love

If you judge people
you have no time
to love them.

Mother Teresa

...when you judge, you cut
off understanding and shut
down the process of
learning to love.

Dr. Deepak Chopra

What is a weed?
A plant whose virtues have
not been discovered.

Ralph Waldo Emerson

The difference between a
flower and a weed
is a judgement.

Anonymous

*Faults can be found even
in saints and angels,
if they are seen through a
judgmental eye.*

TYCHO

*The important thing is not to
think much but
to love much;
and so do that which best
stirs you to love.*

SAINT TERESA OF AVILA

I have learnt
silence from the talkative;
tolerance from the intolerant;
and kindness from the unkind.
I should not be ungrateful
to those teachers.

KAHLIL GIBRAN

Anyone can blame;
it takes a
specialist to praise.

KONSTANTIN STANISLAVSKI

We shouldn't care
about the length of his hair
or the colour of his skin,
don't worry about
what shows from without,
but the love that
lives within.

RAY STEVENS

The essence of love
isn't a feeling
- it is a state of being

DR DEEPAK CHOPRA

Love life as you love your
child, your parent, your
friend, your lover,
and there will be no dream
that cannot be pursued,
nothing hidden that you will
not have the means to find.

ANDREA PHOTIOU

In the final analysis,
we must love in order
not to fall ill.

SIGMUND FREUD

Love one another but make
not a bond of love.
Let there be spaces
in your togetherness.

KAHLIL GIBRAN

If love does not know how
to give and take without
restrictions, it is not love,
but a transaction.

EMMA GOLDMAN

When you set others free
you set yourself free;
when you cling onto others
you hold yourself in a trap.

TYCHO

The arithmetic
of love is unique:
Two halves do not make a
whole; only two wholes
make a whole.

JO COUDERT

If you genuinely love or at least send kind thoughts to a thing, it will change before your eyes.

John and Lyn St Clair Thomas

If we seek to be loved,
if we expect to be loved,
this cannot be accomplished;
We will be
dependent and grasping,
not genuinely loving.

M Scott Peck, MD

Romantic love retards our evolution when it's used as a substitute for our connection to the universal energy.

JAMES REDFIELD / CAROL ADRIENNE

As you increase
your ability to love,
you increase
your ability to heal.

TYCHO

Love that is based on mutual
understanding and respect
will never drain us of our
resources; our fund of love
is replenished even as it
flows out of us,
as though the act of loving
generates more love.

KAREN CASEY / MARTHA VANCEBURG

All you need is love.

LENNON / MCCARTNEY

Love is patient and kind, it
is not jealous or proud.
Love is not selfish or
irritable and does not keep
a record of wrongs.
Love never gives up
and it's faith, hope
and patience never fail.
True love is eternal.

1 Corinthians 13, 1 - 8

There is no difficulty that
enough love will not conquer;
No disease that
enough love will not heal;
No door that
enough love will not open;
No gulf that
enough love will not bridge;
No wall that
enough love will not
throw down;
No sin that
enough love will not redeem....
....If only you could love enough,
you would be the happiest and
most powerful being in the world.

EMMETT FOX

Resolving Conflict

*Man must evolve for all
human conflict, a method
which rejects revenge,
aggression and retaliation.
The foundation of such
a method is love.*

MARTIN LUTHER KING

*Revenge is a strong
human emotion, use it
to your advantage!
Learn forgiveness.*

THOMAS ALLEN.

He who angers you,
conquers you.

ELIZABETH KENNY

Anger repressed can poison a
relationship as surely as
the cruellest words.

JOYCE BROTHERS

He who cannot forgive others breaks the bridge over which he himself must pass one day.

PROVERB

Never in the world is hatred conquered by hatred; hatred is conquered by love.

THE DHAMMAPADA 223.5

An eye for an eye,
a tooth for a tooth....
....and that way
the whole world will be
blind and toothless.

FIDDLER ON THE ROOF

Inner peace can be reached
only when we
practice forgiveness.

GERALD G JAMPOLSKY

Be tolerant with each other and have forgiveness. And to these qualities add love, which binds all things together in perfect unity.

COLOSSIANS 3, 12 - 14

If one's words are no better than silence, then one should remain silent.

THE BUDDHA

The stupid
neither forgive nor forget;
the naive
forgive and forget;
the wise
forgive but do not forget.

THOMAS SZASZ

Whenever we are ill,
we need to look around to
see who it is that we
need to forgive.

A COURSE IN MIRACLES

Imagine there's no countries,
it isn't hard to do.
Nothing to kill or die for,
and no religion too.
Imagine all the people
living life in peace....

JOHN LENNON

Learn From Life

How could we ever discover new territory if we were not lost in the first place?

ANDREA PHOTIOU

It is not our smooth passages that reveal new understandings, but the strenuous, uphill battles that benefit us with the knowledge we need to grow.

KAREN CASEY / MARTHA VANCEBURG

There is none so blind as he who will not see, we must not close our minds, we must let our thoughts be free.

RAY STEVENS

Strive to be self-confident with humbleness, and doubting with openness.

TYCHO

Experience is not what
happens to you;
it is what you do with what
happens to you.

ALDOUS HUXLEY

I know I'm not seeing things
as they are,
I'm seeing things
as I am.

LAUREL LEE

If you shut your door
to all errors,
truth will be shut out.

RABINDRANATH TAGORE

An open mind
allows ideas to flow.
An open heart
allows love to flow.

TYCHO

Reaching out to find the
wonder of the here and now,
hand in hand
with one another,
time will teach us how.

ANDREA PHOTIOU

Everyone and everything
around you is your teacher.

KEN KEYES JR

*One often learns more
from ten days of agony
than from ten years
of contentment.*

MERLE SHAIN

*Sometimes we suffer,
not from the pain itself,
but from the resistance
to the pain.*

TYCHO

Watch that in
your quest for truth,
yourself you don't deceive,
for the answer lies not only
in your eyes, but in what
others too believe.

ANDREA PHOTIOU

The teacher may
have the map,
but the student must
make the journey.

TYCHO

Did you ever wonder how it would feel to be a grub and then turn into a winged creature? It helps us to endure the depressing passage if we can remember that we're being prepared for a new stage of our lives, one in which, perhaps, we will leave our old selves as far behind as the dragonfly leaves the larva.

Karen Casey / Martha Vanceburg

Finding Inner Peace And Happiness

Life is a series of natural
and spontaneous changes.
Don't resist them
- that only creates sorrow.

LAO TZU

Don't try to force anything.
Let life be a deep let-go.
See God opening millions of
flowers everyday without
forcing the buds.

BHAGWAN SHREE RAJNEESH

Just accept life as it is
and go with the flow,
every lesson that you live
tells you what you
need to know.

TYCHO

Row, row, row your boat
gently down the stream;
merrily, merrily, merrily,
merrily, life is but a dream.

CHILD'S NURSERY RHYME

For the root to be out of
order and the branches
to be in order is an
impossibility.

CONFUCIUS.

That the yielding conquers
the resistant and
the soft conquers the hard,
is a fact known by all
but utilised by none.

LAO TZU

To have a crisis,
and act upon it is one thing;
to dwell in perpetual crisis
is another.

BARBARA GRIZZUTI HARRISON

Be in harmony with life at
all times, be at peace with
the world and patiently
accept life as it is.

THE BUDDHA

*Make peace with yourself
and heaven and earth will
make peace with you.*

ST ISAAK OF SYRIA

*True happiness is found
when you have a peaceful
mind and a loving heart.*

TYCHO

The wise man chooses
the path of joy;
the fool takes
the path of pleasure.

KATHA UPANISHAD 2

The greater part of our
happiness or misery depends
on our dispositions and not
on our circumstances.

MARTHA WASHINGTON

Happiness is a road to travel, not a place to be.

PROVERB

Happiness can only be felt if you don't set any condition.

ARTHUR RUBENSTEIN

Happiness is a
by-product of an effort to
make someone else happy.

GRETTA BROOKER PALMER

Acceptance is the key
to freedom from suffering.

TYCHO

When we cling
to pain, we end up
punishing ourselves.

Leo F Buscaglia

Things that appear random
to a limited awareness,
fit into place perfectly when
awareness is expanded.

Dr Deepak Chopra

God, grant me:
the serenity to accept
the things I cannot change;
the courage to change
the things I can,
and the wisdom
to know the difference.

REINHOLD NEIBUHR

All nature is but
art unknown to thee;
All chance, direction which
thou cannot see;
All discord,
harmony not understood;
All partial evil,
universal good;
And, spite of pride,
in erring reason's spite;
One truth is clear,
whatever is, is right.

ALEXANDER POPE

The Law Of Cause And Effect

Actions are like invisible
seeds planted in the unborn.
If the seed is good
the fruit will be good,
if the seed is bad
the fruit will be bad.
Every action of body, speech
and mind is subject to
this natural law.

THE BUDDHA

Whatsoever a man soweth
that shall he also reap.

JESUS CHRIST

No person in the world ever attempted to wrong another without being injured in return - some way, somehow, sometime.

William George Jordan

No thought or action is without results.

The law of karma

Wicked people bring about their own downfall by their evil deeds, but good people are protected by their integrity.

PROVERBS 14, 32

Cease to do evil and purify your heart.

THE BUDDHA

If a man speaks or acts
with an evil thought,
pain follows him.

HINDU PROVERB

The quality
of your life will be
determined by the quality
of your behaviour.

TYCHO

Be generous and
you will be prosperous.
Help others and
you will be helped.

PROVERBS 11, 25

Do as you would
be done by.

RELIGIOUS PROVERB

Don't expect to receive
friendship, love and joy,
if you are giving out
hostility, anger and misery.

TYCHO

People are lonely
because they build walls
instead of bridges.

ANONYMOUS

*The game of life is
a game of boomerangs.
Our thoughts, deeds, and
words return to us
sooner or later,
with astounding accuracy.*

FLORENCE SCOVEL SHINN

*Every action has an equal
and opposite reaction.*

SIR ISAAC NEWTON

A loving person
lives in a loving world,
A hostile person
lives in a hostile world,
Everyone you meet
is your mirror.

KEN KEYES JR

As contagion of
sickness makes sickness,
contagion of trust
can make trust.

MARIANNE MOORE

The only reward of virtue is virtue; the only way to have a friend is to be one.

RALPH WALDO EMERSON

And in the end
the love you take
is equal to
the love you make.

LENNON / MCCARTNEY

Help Whoever You Can

If one could be made to understand that caring only for oneself is bondage while feeding others is freedom, then life would be easy for all.

SHANTANAND SARASWATI

Cultivate great friendliness and great compassion towards all that lives.

THE BUDDHA

*Kind words are like honey -
sweet to the taste and good
for your health.*

PROVERBS 16, 24

*Refrain from false or
malicious speech.*

THE BUDDHA

What you say can preserve life or destroy it; so you must accept the consequences of your words.

PROVERBS 18, 20

The music that can deepest reach, and cure all ill is cordial speech.

EMERSON

Give kind words, be helpful and be consistent between word and deed.

THE BUDDHA

Freely you have given, freely you shall receive.

JESUS CHRIST

Every truth we see is one
to give to the world,
not to keep
to ourselves alone.

ELIZABETH CADY STANTON

Your income is a measure of
how much you are enriching
the lives of others.

TYCHO

You find true joy and happiness in life when you give and give and go on giving and never count the cost.

EILEEN CADDY

If you take much more than you ever give, you end up with less than you started with.

ANDREA PHOTIOU

When we give from a place
of love, rather than from a
place of expectation,
more usually comes back to
us than we could
ever have imagined.

SUSAN JEFFERS

Give a man a fish
and he'll eat for a day,
teach a man to fish
and he'll eat for a life-time.

PROVERB

Do all the good you can,
by all the means you can,
in all the ways you can,
in all the places you can,
at all the times you can,
to all the people you can,
as long as ever you can.

John Wesley

There are two ways
of spreading light:
to be the candle or
the mirror that reflects it.

Edith Wharton

*Perhaps the closest we can
come to a pure gift is an
anonymous one....
Such a gift, which can never
be acknowledged or returned
by those it comforts, can heal
our spirits when they are
wearied by too much ego.*

KAREN CASEY / MARTHA VANCEBURG

Keep Smiling

A smile brings
rest to the weary,
cheer to the discouraged,
sunshine to the sad,
and is nature's best antidote
for trouble.

ANONYMOUS

Laughter is the
best medicine.

PROVERB

Cheerfulness keeps up a kind
of daylight in the mind,
and fills it with a steady and
perpetual serenity.

JOSEPH ADDISON

It's a well-known fact
that the older a man gets,
the faster he could
run as a boy.

ANONYMOUS

*Do not take life
too seriously.
You will never get
out of it alive.*

ELBERT HUBBARD

*I'm not afraid to die.
I just don't want to be there
when it happens.*

WOODY ALLEN

If I could drop dead
right now,
I'd be the happiest
man alive.

SAMUEL GOLDWYN

It is easier to fight for one's
principles than to
live up to them.

ALFRED ADLER

Alas, I know if I ever become truly humble, I would be proud of it.

BENJAMIN FRANKLIN

It is now proved beyond any doubt that smoking is one of the leading causes of statistics.

FLETCHER KNEBEL

Dear God,
I pray for patience.
And I want it right now.

OREN ARNOLD

If only God would give me some clear sign! Like making a large deposit in my name at a Swiss bank.

WOODY ALLEN

Always forgive your enemies,
nothing annoys them
so much.

OSCAR WILDE

I'm just catching up
with yesterday;
by tomorrow I should be
ready for today.

ANONYMOUS

Enjoy Life – Now!

Why does it seem that the
past is always better?
We look back
and we think that:
The winters were warmer,
the grass was greener,
the skies were bluer,
and smiles were bright.
Can it be that it was all so
simple then, or has time
rewritten every line?

SCHMICT-JONES
(*TRY TO REMEMBER*)

*Are you experiencing,
or are you spending most of
your time thinking about
what you experienced or
what you will experience?*

RICHARD HITTLEMAN.

*Here and now
is all we've got.*

THE BUDDHA.

The value of any moment
depends on the consciousness
you bring with it.

Dr. Katherine Watson.

Nothing is worth more
than this day.

Goethe.

The value of ambition
is not in its attainment,
but in the experiences
created while on the
road to attaining it.

TYCHO

Success is a journey not a
destination, half the fun is
just getting there.

GITA BELLIN.

*It is good to have an end
to journey towards;
but it is the journey that
matters in the end.*

URSULA K. LEGUIN.

*Life is what happens to you
while you're busy making
other plans.*

JOHN LENNON.

You can turn to the east,
you can turn to the west,
you can turn to the God
of your choice.
But believe in the right
to believe in yourself,
listen close and you'll hear
your own voice.

ANDREA PHOTIOU

To travel hopefully is
better than to arrive.

SIR JAMES JEANS.

Yesterday's a memory,
tomorrow's still a dream;
and reality lies somewhere
in between.

ANDREA PHOTIOU.

Paradise is where I am.

VOLTAIRE.

BIBLIOGRAPHY

Ageless body, timeless mind, Deepak Chopra. Published by Rider 1993.

Guide to Yoga meditation, Richard Hittleman. Published by Bantam books.

The power of positive thinking, Norman Vincent Peale. Published by Cedar books.

Thorsons introductory guide to Hypnotherapy, Hellmut W. A. Karle. Published by Thorsons 1992.

The promise of a new day, Karen Casey and Martha Vanceburg. Published by Hazelden Meditation series.

Living in the Light, Shakti Gawain. Published by Eden Grove Editions.

The Dynamic Laws of Healing, Catherine Ponder. Published by Devorss & Co.

The Celestine Prophecy, An adventure, James Redfield. Published by Bantam books.

The Celestine Prophecy, An experiential guide, James Redfield and Carol Adrienne. Published by Bantam books.

You can have it all, Arnold Patent. Published by Money Mastery Publishing, 1984.

Feel the fear and do it anyway, Susan Jeffers. Published by Arrow books limited.

Yoga, Hari Prasad Shastri. Published by W&G Foyle Ltd.

A guide for the advanced soul, Susan Hayward. Published by In-tune books.

Eyes of the beholder, John and Lyn St. Clair-Thomas/Steven Shackel. Published by Angel Publications.

The nature of personal reality, Jane Roberts. Published by Prentice Hall, Inc.

A Course in miracles. Published by Foundation for inner peace.

The Dawn of change, Eileen Caddy. Published by The Findhorn press.

God spoke to me, Eileen Caddy. Published by The Findhorn press.

A mans wisdom can
be measured, not by what
he knows nor what
he says but by how he lives.
To live wisely means
to live lovingly.

TYCHO